SUFFOLK BUSES

JOHN LAW

AMBERLEY

A typical market day scene in the coach park at Bury St Edmunds, *circa* 1976. Vehicles from Premier Travel, Towler's of Brandon, Soames and Sons of Ipswich, and Theobald's of Long Melford are visible.

First published 2017

Amberley Publishing
The Hill, Stroud
Gloucestershire, GL5 4EP

www.amberley-books.com

Copyright © John Law, 2017

The right of John Law to be identified as
the Author of this work has been asserted in
accordance with the Copyrights, Designs and
Patents Act 1988.

ISBN 978 1 4456 6810 9 (print)
ISBN 978 1 4456 6811 6 (ebook)

British Library Cataloguing in Publication Data.
A catalogue record for this book is available from
the British Library.

Typesetting by Amberley Publishing.
Printed in the UK.

Introduction

The county of Suffolk forms the southern half of what is properly regarded as East Anglia. Contrary to conventional thinking, the area is not flat; indeed, Suffolk consists mainly of undulating terrain, except for the estuarial regions. The county is largely rural, with several small towns such as Aldeburgh and Southwold on the coast and Stowmarket, Framlingham, and Newmarket further inland. Ipswich, the largest conurbation, is the county town, while Bury St Edmunds comes second. Lowestoft, close to the Norfolk border, is an important harbour, though much busier today is the vast container port of Felixstowe.

Like much of the country, public transport began with the local farmers using their horse-drawn carts to convey people into the nearby towns on market days. More sophisticated methods of getting Suffolk's population into urban centres began in 1880, when a horse tramway opened in Ipswich. This private company was taken over by Ipswich Corporation in 1899, with the system being electrified in 1903. The municipality's public transport system remained all electric until 1950, when motorbuses were introduced.

Meanwhile, Lowestoft Corporation also introduced trams, when the one route – using electric vehicles – opened in 1903. Motorbuses began service here in 1927 and the small tram system was made redundant four years later.

With only two municipal operators in the county, the major bus operator became Eastern Counties Omnibus Co. Ltd (ECOC) in 1931. This had been formed by way of a merger between the similarly named Eastern Counties Road Car Company (based in Suffolk), Ortona Motor Company of Cambridgeshire, Peterborough Electric Tramways, and the East Anglian operations of United Automobile Services.

The Transport Act of 1947 brought nationalisation to much of Britain's bus industry, with ECOC becoming part of the Tilling Group. More political manoeuvrings saw the formation of the National Bus Company in 1969, with ECOC becoming a significant part and the Tilling red and cream livery becoming replaced by standard NBC colours.

After the election of Margaret Thatcher, the Eastern Counties Omnibus Co. Ltd was split up, with newly formed Cambus taking over the western operations of the area. Cambus eventually sold out to the Stagecoach Group and that company's buses can still be found today in Suffolk, with an operation around Newmarket and an express service into Bury St Edmunds.

The rest of ECOC became the subject of a management buyout in 1987, selling out to the GRT Group in 1994, which soon became part of First Bus. Today that company is in charge of the majority of bus operations in Suffolk.

The fate of the two municipal operators – Lowestoft and Ipswich – could not be more different. Lowestoft Corporation Transport became the property of Waveney District Council in 1974 and, after a failed co-ordination scheme with Eastern Counties, sold out to that business in 1977.

Ipswich Corporation Transport remained in council hands throughout, though it is now an 'arm's length' company called Ipswich Buses. Today it is one of only a handful of such operations in the United Kingdom. At one time, negotiations were ongoing to sell out to the Go Ahead Group, but these did not come to fruition.

The rural nature of Suffolk has long meant that it is fertile ground for the independent bus sector. These have varied from the one-bus operation of J. Amos and Son from Belchamp St Paul to the large company, Premier Travel, who ran several services in West Suffolk. Both companies are, today, no longer trading.

Several well-known bus companies have recently sold out to the Go Ahead Group, including Chambers of Bures, Hedingham Omnibuses, and Anglian Coaches, all of who run services within Suffolk, with each retaining its own identity.

Ipswich Buses have expanded their operations beyond the town's boundaries, partly through the tendering process and also by taking over services from companies such as Squirell's of Hitcham and Bicker's of Coddenham.

Nevertheless, independent companies still make up a good proportion of the county's bus routes. Simonds of Botesdale have long operated the Bury St Edmunds to Norwich route and continue to do so today. Galloway of Mendlesham has seen an expansion of their stage carriage duties. Essex independents Regal Busways and Stephensons now regularly operate into the county.

Altogether, the Suffolk bus scene provides a great variety of operators and colour schemes for today's bus enthusiasts and photographers – long may that situation continue.

Finally, thanks to Richard Huggins for providing a few photographs at unusual location, and to Bus Lists on the Web for providing a 'one-stop-shop' during the research for this publication.

Eastern Counties was the major operator throughout Suffolk. Formerly a member of the Tilling Group, it had a standard fleet of buses by the time it became part of the National Bus Company. Pre-NBC livery is still applied to all the saloons illustrated in this early 1970s photograph, taken at Bury St Edmunds depot. On the left is number RL502 (APW 502J) – a Bristol RELL6G with ECW fifty-three-seat bus body – while similar RLE862 (WNG 862H) has fifty dual-purpose seats and the appropriate livery. Sandwiched between the two, against the depot wall, is earlier LM472 (472 BNG); a 1963-built Bristol MW5G with ECW bodywork seating forty-five.

The rear-loading double-decker lasted quite a while in the Eastern Counties fleet, well into National Bus Company days. As late as 20 June 1981, number LFS72 (72 DPW) is seen passing the old railway crossing cottage en route to Kirkley in the suburbs of Lowestoft. This seventy-seat Bristol FS5G/ECW bus, fitted with platform doors, had been new to Eastern Counties in 1963. Thanks to Richard Huggins for supplying this photograph.

Like the company's buses, the Eastern Counties coach fleet mainly consisted of Bristol/ECW manufacture. Number LS828 (APW 828B) is no exception, being an MW6G with coach bodywork in National white livery, capable of carrying thirty-nine seated passengers. It is seen in the yard of Bury St Edmunds depot, *circa* 1977.

Later deliveries of half-cab double-deckers saw Eastern Counties receive batches of Bristol FLF6G buses, such as this fine pair, both new in 1966. Numbers FLF440 and FLF441 (GPW 440/1D) are both seen in the Old Cattle Market bus station in Ipswich in 1980. As can be seen, the company's depot was alongside in those days.

Sometime around 1977, when Eastern Counties had their own bus station in the centre of Bury St Edmunds, fleet number VR163 (MCL 939P) is having a rest beside the company's offices. This Bristol VRT/SL3/6LXB with seventy-four-seat bodywork by ECW had been new in 1976. At the time, the independent bus companies serving the town had to make do with Angel Hill as a starting point for their services, but the 1990s saw the opening of a new bus station, used by all operators.

Another photograph taken at the Old Cattle Market bus station in Ipswich in 1980, which was used mainly by Eastern Counties. Posing for the camera is Leyland National number LN783 (DPW 783T) – a forty-nine-seat bus of standard National Bus Company fleets, apart from the unusual wrap-round advertisement extolling the virtues of joining the British Army. Alongside in full NBC red is Bristol VR/ECW VR332 (NAG 587G), which had come from Scottish operator Western SMT.

Delivered in 1979, Bristol VRT/SL3/6LXB number VR242 (JAH 242V) with the normal ECW seventy-four-seat layout is seen through the lens of Richard Huggins' camera on 29 March 1981. Appropriately it is seen outside the Bristol Arms at Shotley Pier, owned by Ipswich brewers Tolly Cobbold at the time. From here there were fine views across the Stour estuary to Harwich and Felixstowe. The pub's name does not derive from the bus outside, but because it was owned by the Marquis of Bristol in the early nineteenth century.

Back at the Old Cattle Market bus station in Ipswich, this time in 1983, here is Eastern Counties fleet number RE849 (RPU 869M). This 1974-built Bristol RELH6G with ECW coach bodywork seating forty-seven passengers had been delivered new to National Travel (South East) for its Essex operations. Despite retaining its white coaching livery, it appears to be being used on stage carriage duties.

Another picture taken in the Old Cattle Market bus station in Ipswich, again in 1983, though on a different occasion from the last one. Eastern Counties number LL753 (MCL 935P) has dual-purpose livery, applied in rather an unusual variety of NCB corporate colours. This vehicle is one of a batch of Leyland Leopards with Alexander 'T' type forty-nine-seat dual-purpose bodies, delivered to ECOC in 1976.

With a long North Sea coastline, it will come as no surprise to learn that open-top bus services are popular in Eastern Suffolk. Seen at Felixstowe Docks terminus on 2 July 1984 is Eastern Counties number OT2 (VDV 753); a 1957-built Bristol LDL6G/ECW bus that had been new to Western National as fleet number 1936, long before it had been converted to open-top. The bus appears to be heading for Bawdsey Ferry. Alongside is standard Bristol VR number VR189 (RPW 189R) on the Ipswich service. Photograph by Richard Huggins.

Another open-topper in the Eastern Counties fleet, number OT3 (JNG 50N), is seen inside the small depot in central Ipswich in late 1986. This Bristol VRT/SL6G had been new to ECOC in 1975 with a standard roofed seventy-four-seat ECW body. It had originally been given fleet number VR152.

1986 saw the closure of Eastern Counties' Lowestoft depot, located on London Road. Richard Huggins photographed the facility on 26 July 1986, when it appeared to be occupied by Scottish Citylink coaches and a second-hand Bristol VR. ECOC's own vehicles have been left exposed to the elements in the yard.

Close to the Essex border is the sizeable village of East Bergholt, birthplace of the artist John Constable. Eastern Counties maintained an outstation here, where three buses are seen on 18 August 1985. Bristol VR types VR127 (RAH 127M) and VR192 (TEX 402R), both seventy-four-seaters, are seen alongside saloon number LH922 (TCL 142R). This forty-three-seat Bristol LH6L/ECW had been new to ECOC in 1977. This particular parking area was redeveloped in 1988, with buses moving to another location in the village. The outstation finally closed in 1998. Photograph by Richard Huggins.

Another 1985 photograph by Richard Huggins, taken on 26 November, at Ridley Road, on the Westley Estate in Bury St Edmunds – terminus of route 953. On service on that day was Eastern Counties number RL674 (PPW 674F); a Bristol RELL6G of 1968 construction, with an ECW bus body seating fifty-three passengers.

The small Eastern Counties depot in Lowestoft, at Gordon Road, played host to a fleet of minibuses during the later years of the 1980s. At that location, on 26 July 1986, is Freight Rover Sherpa number SD642 (C642 BEX), which was only a month or two old at the time. This vehicle, seating sixteen passengers in a Dormobile body, is pictured by Richard Huggins as it departs from the garage to take up a service to Oulton.

The 1977 batch of Eastern Counties Bristol LH6L saloons were withdrawn in 1988. Operating a special tour commemorating the event, on 18 December of that year, is number LH922 (TCL 142R) – (*see page 11*). The location is the village of Grundisburgh, a few miles inland from Woodbridge. The church of St Mary's is to the right, said to date back to the fourteenth century, though the brick-built tower was constructed in the 1730s. To the left of the bus is the village's old school, since replaced by a new construction. Photograph by Richard Huggins.

We return to the Old Cattle Market bus station in Ipswich, to see Eastern Counties VR287 (VEX 287X) in the spring of 1985. Originally ordered by Alder Valley, this Bristol VRT/SL3/6LXB with ECW bodywork was fitted with dual-purpose seating, hence the unusual application of NBC colours.

The famous racing town of Newmarket is firmly in Suffolk, despite it being almost surrounded by Cambridgeshire. It came as no surprise that, upon Eastern Counties being split up in preparation for privatisation, the Newmarket operations and depot passed to Cambus. Nevertheless, ECOC retained a presence in the town, using the Cambus depot as an outstation. Seen here on 26 November 1985 is an early Bristol VRT/SL6G with ECW seventy-seat bodywork; number VR401 (OCK 101K). This bus had been new to Ribble Motor Services as number 2001 in 1972. Alongside is a later Cambus Bristol VR, number 623 (SNG 437M), which had started life with ECOC as fleet number VR137. Photograph by Richard Huggins.

A most unusual coach in the Eastern Counties fleet is number CB812 (PBJ 706R), a 1976-built Bedford YMT/Duple Dominant fifty-three-seat coach to bus grant specification (with folding doors for stage service duties). It had been new to an Ipswich independent, Sayers Coaches. It later passed to Bickers of Coddenham, a business taken over by Ipswich Buses in 1988. It is seen with a good load of mature ladies heading for Bawdsey as it departs from the Old Cattle Market in Ipswich, spring 1989.

Probably on the same occasion as the above photograph, Eastern Counties number LL792 (OEX 792W) leaves Ipswich for Colchester. One of several Willowbrook-bodied forty-nine-seat Leyland Leopards received by ECOC in 1980, it is seen here painted in the post-National Bus Company livery.

As part of the Government's privatisation plans, Ambassador Travel was formed as a National Bus Company subsidiary, being formed from the coaching arm of Eastern Counties. Fleet number RE845 (LWC 980J) – a 1971-built Bristol RELH6G/Plaxton Elite forty-seven-seat coach – is seen at ECOC's Newmarket outstation (the Cambus depot) on 2 February 1985. The coach was one of six transferred from National Travel (South East) in 1978. Photograph by Richard Huggins.

One of the first buses ordered by the newly privatised Eastern Counties Omnibus Company was number S17 (H617 RAH). This Dennis Javelin, delivered in late 1990, has a Plaxton bus body to dual-purpose specification, seating fifty-one passengers. Resplendent in its new colours, it is seen entering the Old Cattle Market bus station in Ipswich, passing the very convenient Plough pub on Dog's Head Street in summer 1991.

Following the management buyout from the National Bus Company in 1987, Eastern Counties was sold to the GRT Group in 1994. Just over a year later the GRT Group merged with Badgerline to form Firstbus. Around the time of that event, in the summer of 1995, number VR243 (JAH 243V), a Bristol VRT/SL3/6LXB with seventy-four-seat ECW bodywork, is seen on its stance in the Old Cattle Market bus station in Ipswich, in the current livery of the time.

Another Bristol VR photographed in the summer of 1995, number OT353 (JNG 50N), is seen near Ipswich railway station, heading for Shotley on route 97. Originally fleet number VR152, delivered to ECOC in 1975, this VRT/SL6G was fitted with an ECW H43/31F body but was later converted to open top.

Another photograph taken in the summer of 1995, about the time of the formation of Firstbus. Eastern Counties number IC83 (F710NJF), an Iveco 49.10 minibus with twenty-five-seat Carlyle bodywork, is seen in the Old Cattle Market bus station in Ipswich. This vehicle had been new to Leicester City Transport and had been transferred during the period of GRT ownership of both companies.

Again, it is the summer of 1995 and Eastern Counties number DP77 (M377 YEX) is seen opposite the entrance to the Old Cattle Market bus station in Ipswich, on Dog's Head Street, with the Buttermarket shopping centre behind. This thirty-four-seat Dennis Dart/Plaxton bus is fitted with guide wheels for operating on the short guided busway section of 'Superoute' 66, which had been introduced during the previous year.

Now branded as First Eastern Counties, two Leyland Olympians with ECW bodywork bask in the winter sun at the Old Cattle Market bus station in Ipswich in February 1999. Both had been recently transferred in from other operators in the Firstbus organisation. Closest to the camera, number 98 (KGG 157Y) had been new to Strathclyde PTE (who became First Glasgow), while number 102 (XHK 236X) had been new to Eastern National in 1981.

Another transfer within the Firstbus Group was that of Wright bodied Dennis Dart twenty-six-seater bus JDZ 2319. It had been new to London Buses in 1991 as number DW19, where it had been used on 'Gold Arrow' service from Westbourne Park Garage. On privatisation it passed to Centrewest – a company taken over by Firstbus in 1997. It was transferred to First Eastern Counties a year or so later and given fleet number 490, as seen at the new Bury St Edmunds bus station in February 1999, operating a local service. This vehicle was later transferred to Ipswich depot, where it later gained corporate fleet number 45319.

In the mid-1990s, Eastern Counties had a total of sixteen of their Leyland National buses rebuilt by East Lancs to 'Greenway' standard. One of them, fleet number 661 (NIL 3961), is seen under Firstbus ownership at Bury St Edmunds in February 1999. Originally number LN599 in the ECOC fleet, registered WVF 599S, this fifty-two-seater received the 'Greenway' treatment in 1995.

Transferred within the Firstbus Group, from Yorkshire Rider, Volvo B6-50/Alexander 'Dash' forty-seater L106 PWR is seen departing from the Old Cattle Market bus station in Ipswich in February 1999. Given fleet number 399 for its East Anglia period, it was number 3006 when operating in West Yorkshire.

Suffolk Buses

First Eastern Counties number MG111 (N611 GAH) was delivered in August 1995. This Mercedes 609D minibus, with Frank Guy twenty-seat bodywork, was found at work in central Lowestoft on a local duty in February 1999.

First Group's 'Barbie' livery began to be applied to the former Eastern Counties fleet sometime around 2000. The policy, at first, was only to paint vehicles that met modern standards – i.e. low-floor. Seen in those colours is number 596 (W596 SNG), a Scania L94UB with forty-three-seat Wright bodywork, at Sudbury bus station on a lovely summer's day in 2000. The tower of St Peter's Church is prominent in the background; now redundant, but a listed building and still in use for other community purposes.

A simplified version of Firstbus livery is seen applied to number 386 in the Eastern Counties fleet, seen in Dog's Head Street, Ipswich, in March 2004. Registered L101 WYS, this Volvo B6-50 with Alexander 'Dash' forty-seat bus had been new to Kelvin Central, in Scotland, where it carried fleet number 1021.

At the same location as the above photograph, but on 6 May 2016, we see Firstbus number 66850 (MX05 CHD), proudly wearing its localised corporate livery, on service 61 to the suburb of Greenwich. This Volvo B7RLE saloon, with forty-three-seat Wright bodywork, had been new to First Group's operations in Greater Manchester, where it had carried the same fleet number – demonstrating the advantages of a national numbering scheme.

The county of Suffolk had two municipal operators, one of which, Ipswich, still survives. The other, Lowestoft Corporation Transport (later to become Waveney District Council) lasted until 1977. Like many council-owned bus enterprises, that in Lowestoft began with trams. Basically, the system had one route – from Yarmouth Road to Pakefield, plus a mile-long branch, giving a total of four miles of track. Here, car number 7 – built by Milnes of Birkenhead in 1903 – crosses the swing bridge over the harbour entrance, just south of the town centre. The tram operations were abandoned in 1931, to be replaced by motorbuses. One tram survives in the East Anglia Transport Museum in Carlton Colville.

Lowestoft Corporation Transport's bus fleet was certainly not without interest. The late Les Flint visited the town on 21 June 1965, when he found number 26 (GBJ 197) passing along London Road North in the town centre. This 1947-built AEC Regent II had locally built ECW bodywork, seating fifty-six passengers. It was finally withdrawn as late as 1971.

Throughout its history, Lowestoft Corporation Transport had purchased Guys and AECs for its bus needs. However, in 1965, the first of four Leyland PD2A/30 double-deckers, number 9 (BRT 668C), was purchased. Carrying Massey H34/28R bodywork, this bus is seen in the depot yard in 1973.

1974 saw Lowestoft Corporation Transport become Waveney District Council, though the brown and cream colour scheme was retained. The last of the Leyland double-deckers to be purchased by LCT was number 12 (PBJ 2F), a PD2/47 of 1967 construction. Again, Massey sixty-two-seat bodywork is fitted. It is seen in the depot yard displaying the council's new logo in 1977 – the year that Waveney District Council ceased operating buses.

In 1969 Lowestoft Corporation Transport bought a batch of four unusual AEC Swifts with ECW forty-five-seat dual-doorway bodies. The last of the batch, Waveney DC number 4 (YRT 898H), is seen leaving the small depot building in 1977. This bus has since been preserved and restored to the livery it carried as new. Two similar buses, new in 1974, passed to Great Yarmouth Transport when Waveney DC gave up its bus operations in 1977.

In 1970, two buses were purchased from Great Yarmouth Corporation for operation in the Lowestoft Corporation Transport fleet. In Waveney DC days, number 5 (AEX 82B) is seen in the depot. New as GYT number 82, this saloon is a rare example of a Massey-bodied short AEC Reliance, seating thirty-nine passengers.

No excursion to Lowestoft in the 1970s was complete without a visit to the premises of Eastern Coach Works. Most of the construction work was visible from the public road alongside, while the yard outside was used to park completed vehicles. In the summer of 1973, brand new SELNEC (the predecessor to Great Manchester Transport) number 65 (AWH 65L) is ready for despatch. This Leyland Leopard was fitted with forty-nine coach seats.

A much more standard bus outside the Eastern Coach Works factory in Lowestoft is PRU 917R, a Bristol VRT/SL3/6LXB, newly fitted with this seventy-four-seat body. It is seen in late 1976, ready for delivery to Hants and Dorset, where it would become fleet number 3358. A similar bus – albeit with Leyland engine – PEH 653R, is behind, destined to become Potteries Motor Traction number 653.

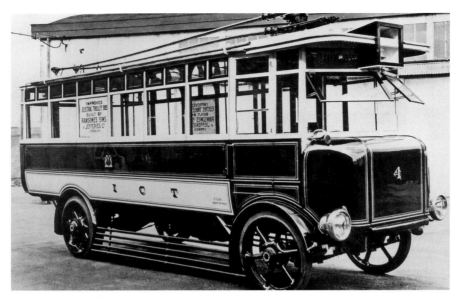

Municipal transport in Ipswich started in 1901, when the Corporation purchased the town's horse tram network in 1901. Electric trams took over from the horses in 1903, but the trams did not last too long, with all routes being replaced by trolleybuses by 1926. The Railless Company built the first three trolleybuses delivered, but local company Ransomes, Sims and Jefferies constructed number 4 in the fleet. Seen when brand new in 1924, it was later registered DX 4648. It was capable of carrying thirty seated passengers.

From 1926 until 1950, Ipswich Corporation's only passenger-carrying vehicles consisted solely of trolleybuses. Karrier of Huddersfield supplied most post-war deliveries. However, the last trolleybuses delivered were numbers 115 to 126, badged as Sunbeams, to the F4 design. Fifty-six-seat Park Royal bodywork was fitted, as seen on this preserved example – number 126 (ADX 196), seen under the wires of the Sandtoft Transport Centre (as it was then known), near Doncaster, in 1980. It has since returned to Suffolk, joining other trolleybuses at the Ipswich Transport Museum.

The first Ipswich Corporation motor buses were delivered in 1950, consisting of six AEC Regent III /Park Royal double-deckers. In all, a total of sixteen were received; the last one being built in 1956. The later ones survived into 1974, with number 24 (EPV 24) becoming a driver training vehicle. It is seen in that year passing the now-closed Falcon pub, on, appropriately, Falcon Street, in the town centre.

Following on from the Regent III deliveries, Ipswich Corporation ordered a dozen AEC Regent V buses, with Park Royal sixty-five-seat bodies, to assist in trolleybus replacement. The final trolleys were withdrawn in 1963. Number 30 (GPV 30), which entered the fleet in 1958, is seen in the company of similar buses in Lloyds Avenue in the town centre.

Ipswich Corporation also received some AEC single-deckers, the first one being number 7 (BPV 7), delivered in 1953. The bus, an AEC Regal IV with forty-two-seat dual-doorway bodywork by Park Royal, is seen in Lloyds Avenue, very close to the Electric House terminus in 1974.

As the run-down of the trolleybus system continued, many more AEC Regent V buses were ordered, with bodywork by East Lancashire Coachworks. Number 60 (ADX 60) was new in 1960 as a sixty-five-seater, though the bodywork was built by Neepsend – a subsidiary of East Lancs, but based in Sheffield. Standing behind is number 79 (JRT 79K), an AEC Swift with Willowbrook B40D body. The location is the Electric House bus terminus in the town centre, in 1976. The municipal buses of Ipswich have long used Electric House as a bus station – a situation still in place today, though it is now known as Tower Ramparts.

The year 1967 saw four AEC Reliance saloons being purchased by Ipswich Corporation. One of these, number 69 (HPV 69F), with Massey forty-seat dual-doorway bodywork, is arriving at Electric House bus station in 1978, overtaking AEC Swift number 81.

The introduction of rear-engined double-deck buses into the UK market meant that Ipswich Corporation was obliged to obtain the type from a source other than AEC. So, in 1968, a batch of four Leyland Atlantean PDR1/1 vehicles, with seventy-four-seat ECW bodies, came into the fleet. Numerically the second to be received, number 74 (LDX 74G) is seen at Electric House in 1980.

Later deliveries of Leyland Atlanteans to Ipswich Buses carried Roe seventy-two-seat bodies, to dual-door configuration. Number 21 (SDX 21R), to AN68A/1R specification, is seen loading up at Electric House in 1980. It is painted in a special tramway livery to commemorate one hundred years of public transport in the town.

Another Leyland Atlantean (AN68/1R) with Roe bodywork, delivered in 1976, number 9 (MRT 9P) is seen in a different version of tramway livery, cut down to become an open-topper. It is photographed opposite the Electric House terminus in the summer of 1995. It is operating a special tourist service connecting the parks, the historic docks and the old Tolly Cobbold brewery with the town centre.

The year 1980 saw Ipswich Borough Transport purchase its first second-hand buses; four ex-West Yorkshire Passenger Transport Executive Roe-bodied Leyland Atlantean PDR2/1 double-deckers. Still bearing its WYPTE colours is number 41 (UNW 401H), seen inside the depot (near Portman Road football ground) in 1981.

Another source of pre-owned buses was Leicester City Transport. Number 121 (TRY 121H) was one of five Bristol RELL6L/ECW B47D saloons bought in 1980. It is seen at Electric House in 1981.

The last Leyland Atlanteans bought by Ipswich Borough Transport were numbers 37 to 40, new in 1981. The first of these AN68C/1R 'deckers, with East Lancs seventy-three-seat bodies, is number 37 (RGV 37W) – seen at the Bristol Arms in Shotley on 21 April 1985. Photograph by Richard Huggins.

The Dennis Falcon single-decker first entered the Ipswich fleet in 1985. Seven more appeared in the year after. Number 109 (C109 SDX) of that batch is seen at Electric House/Tower Ramparts in late 1986. Northern Counties supplied the body, with two doorways and forty-four bus seats. Like many of the vehicles in the fleet at the time, it carries a name – in this case, *Merlin*.

An unusual vehicle for a council-owned bus business, this Bova integral coach was new in 1982 as VWX 354X to Wallace Arnold, the famous tour operator from Leeds. Reregistered to IXI 5228 and given fleet number 330, it is seen here in the hands of Ipswich Borough Transport at the depot in mid-1989.

New to Ipswich Borough Transport in 1994 was number 183 (L183 APV), a DAF SB220/Optare Delta forty-four-seater, fitted with dual-doorway. It is seen at Tower Ramparts bus station in the year of its delivery.

In 1988 a much-loved independent, Bickers of Coddenham, sold its vehicles and services to Eastern Counties and Ipswich Buses. With the latter, as number 171 (UFT 928T), in March 1990, is this Bedford YMT/Plaxton Supreme Express fifty-three-seat coach. It had been new in 1979 to Northumberland operator Rochester and Marshall. It is about to depart from the Old Cattle Market bus station in Ipswich on a rural route to Debenham.

Ipswich Buses fleet number 41 (M41 EPV), named *May*, is seen at Tower Ramparts bus station in the summer of 1995. Almost new when photographed, this Volvo Olympian carries East Lancs eighty-seat bodywork, to the usual dual-door configuration.

With the takeover of Bickers of Coddenham, and also Squirrell's of Hitcham, the green vehicles of Ipswich Buses appeared in the Suffolk countryside on a regular basis. On one such working is number 119 (G119 VDX), a Dennis Falcon with East Lancs B45D bodywork. Named *Lady Jean*, it is seen in the small town of Bildeston in summer 1991. In the left background is the Kings Head pub, which brewed its own beer at the time.

Similar to the above bus, this Dennis Falcon/East Lancs bus, Ipswich number 143 (TWJ 343Y), was new as a fifty-two-seater to Chesterfield Transport in 1983. Given the name *Haste Away*, it is seen at the Old Cattle Market bus station in the company of number 121 (G121 VDX), named *Nautilus*, in summer 1991.

In 1985 Ipswich Buses purchased some new Bristol B21 saloons, a rare breed on the UK mainland. Following the success of these vehicles, five more were purchased second-hand from Northern Ireland in 1992. Three of them are see at the Old Cattle Market bus station in March 1994. Closest to the camera is number 149 (TDX 124W), with Alexander fifty-three seat bodywork, new as WOI 3002 with Belfast Citybus. Alongside are identical numbers 151 and 152, which had been built for Ulsterbus. Ipswich Buses used them on rural routes.

Ipswich Buses number 161 (L161 ADX) is seen having a rest at Tower Ramparts terminus in the town centre in March 1994. This Dennis Lance, new at the time, has East Lancs forty-one-seat bodywork.

Another visit to Tower Ramparts, in February 1999, found Ipswich Buses number 44 (C722 NNN), a second-hand purchase from Trent Motor Traction. In that fleet it had been number 722, a Leyland Olympian of 1985 vintage with ECW bodywork seating seventy-five passengers.

The low-floor bus arrived in Ipswich Buses in 1997, with a batch of Optare Excel saloons and five East Lancs-bodied Dennis Dart SLF single-deckers. Of the latter, number 134 (R134 FBJ), with dual-doorway and seating thirty-nine passengers, passes the Cricketers public house in February 1999. This fine establishment, situated across Crown Street from Tower Ramparts bus station, is seen as a Wetherspoon's outlet, but had been built for local brewers Tolly Cobbold.

Passing along Crown Street in Ipswich town centre in February 1999 is Ipswich Buses number 50 (P442 SWX). This DAF DB250/Optare Spectra seventy-nine-seater – one of the first low-floor double-deck types in the UK – had been built for Istanbul, Turkey, but the order was cancelled prior to delivery. This accounts for the Yorkshire registration, where the bus was completed, at Crossgates, near Leeds.

Another product of the Leeds factory was the Optare Metrorider; a modernised design of the erstwhile MCW version. Altogether, Ipswich Buses purchased sixteen of these vehicles. One example, number 222 (G222 VDX), named *Mimas* after one of Saturn's moons, is seen at Tower Ramparts in early 1990. The bus was capable of carrying thirty-one seated passengers.

Park and Ride services have become popular in Ipswich in recent years, as the medieval streets of the town centre do not make driving there easy. Painted in a special livery for those duties is Ipswich Buses number 187 (R187 DDX), a thirty-seven-seat Optare Excel integral saloon, fitted with just a single doorway. It is seen passing the Cricketers pub on Crown Street in February 1999.

Also in the distinctive Park and Ride livery is Ipswich Buses number 55 (PN52 XBO), a DAF DE02 'decker with East Lancs H43/28F bodywork. It is seen on Dog's Head Street in the town centre, in March 2004.

Ipswich Buses certainly have bought a good variety of buses over the years. Number 60 (PJ54 YZT) is a Scania N94UD with low-floor East Lancs eighty-seat single-doorway bodywork. Seen at Tower Ramparts 8 May 2007, it is named *Olaf Tryggvason*, after the King of Norway from AD 995 to 1000.

In recent years it has been the policy of Ipswich Buses to specify only single-doored buses. An example of this is fleet number 85 (PJ53 OLE), a Transbus Dennis Dart with East Lancs forty-one-seat bodywork, new in late 2003. It is seen operating the Martlesham Park and Ride service in Dog's Head Street, stopping by the Buttermarket shopping centre, in March 2004.

Delivered in 2002 to Ipswich Buses as fleet number 54 (PN52 XBM), this vehicle was renumbered as 100 when it received this special gold livery to mark one hundred years of buses in the town. The DAF DE02/East Lancs bus is seen departing from Tower Ramparts on 6 May 2016.

Ipswich Buses H775 PTW started life with Dublin Bus, registered 90 D 1028, as a dual-doored Leyland Olympian with bodywork by Alexander (Belfast). It is seen in an interim colour scheme, converted to single-door and without fleet number visible, at Tower Ramparts, 8 May 2007. This bus later received the standard green livery and was given fleet number 39.

Another second-hand bus that had started life with a dual-doorway layout. Ipswich Buses number 13 (LG02 FDF), a Dennis Trident/Alexander 'decker, had been new to London United in 2002. It is seen in Dog's Head Street, Ipswich town centre, 31 March 2011.

Ipswich Buses introduced a new livery around 2013, as seen on number 72 (YN56 NVD); photographed at Tower Ramparts on 6 May 2016. This 2007-built all Scania N94UB carries thirty-six-seat bodywork. Sadly, the policy of giving each bus a name seems to have been abandoned.

Another Scania bus in the Ipswich Buses fleet is number 69 (YJ60 KGY). The N230UD chassis carries an Optare body, seating seventy-four passengers. It is seen leaving Tower Ramparts on 6 May 2016.

Also photographed on 6 May 2016, but in Dog's Head Street, is Ipswich Buses number 104 (SN16 OGK), which had been delivered only two months previously. Introducing a new marque to the fleet, it is an Alexander Dennis E20D Enviro, with thirty-nine-seat bodywork by the same company.

Despite a good number of recent new purchases, Ipswich Buses have continued to buy quality second-hand vehicles. From the London operations of Stagecoach has come number 143 (Y294 FJN), a Dennis Dart SLF/Alexander saloon, converted to single-door before entering service in Suffolk. Tower Ramparts bus station, 6 May 2016.

Another new type of bus recently purchased by Ipswich Buses is the Mercedes Citaro, with the latest style of Mercedes forty-seat bodywork. Number 153 (BF65 HVT) is seen in Tower Ramparts bus station, again on 6 May 2016.

One make of chassis that never made it into the Ipswich Buses fleet was the MAN 18-240. However, the business did try one out, as evidenced by this shot of demonstrator CU56 AVP on loan in Dog's Head Street on 8 May 2007. The bus carried East Lancs forty-three-seat bodywork.

When Eastern Counties was split up in the 1980s, Cambus was formed to take over the Cambridgeshire operations. This meant the occasional foray into Suffolk, with the X11 from Cambridge to Bury St Edmunds. Arriving in the latter town in March 1993 is this rare beast, number 506 (B144 GSC). It had been new to Eastern Scottish as a coach-seated Leyland Olympian, with an unusual style of Alexander bodywork.

Cambus sold out to the Stagecoach Group in 1995. Bearing that company's distinctive livery is number 979 (M959 VWY) – a twenty-nine-seat Optare Metrorider – seen at Newmarket's small bus station in February 1999.

Owned by Tellings-Golden Miller at the time – spring 2005 – Network Colchester had gained a few tendered routes outside the Essex town. Still carrying its Arriva (who took over Colchester Transport) number of E4335, J56 GCX is seen in Bury St Edmunds. It is a DAF SB220 with Ikarus bodywork, which had been new to Hughes DAF, who had loaned it to Strathclyde Buses.

Another operator from the Cambridge area that ran into Suffolk was Premier Travel. Seen at Angel Hill, Bury St Edmunds, *circa* 1975, is 326 NJO, an ex-City of Oxford 1963-built AEC Bridgemaster with Park Royal bodywork seating sixty-five passengers.

Premier Travel also maintained a depot in Suffolk, at the town of Haverhill. VDV 794 is seen there, just after withdrawal, sometime around 1974. New to Devon General in 1957, it is an AEC Reliance/Weymann saloon forty-one-seater.

Burton's Coaches, based at Haverhill, was part of the Tellings-Golden Miller empire in spring 1995 when this photograph was taken at Bury St Edmunds. R70 BCL, a Dennis Dart SLF/ Caetano forty-seat saloon, new to Burton's, was originally registered HX51 LRL. The Burton's business was sold by TGM in 2010 and no longer trades.

Another Burton's bus, given fleet number 800, N540 TPF, is seen resting at Bury St Edmunds bus station on 26 August 2009. It had been new as a Dennis Dart with East Lancs forty-seat bodywork to London & Country in 1995.

The village of Nayland lies on the north bank of the River Stour, the watercourse marking the border with Essex. Nayland was the home to Norfolk's Coaches, with a yard and a separate depot building in the heart of the village. Seen in the yard, *circa* 1973, are FDB 575 and VVF 539. The former, a Burlingham-bodied Leyland Tiger Cub, had been new to North Western Road Car Company. The bus on the right, a Bristol SC4LK/ECW, was originally number LC539 in the Eastern Counties fleet.

Norfolk's main bus route was southwards to Colchester and that is where DEB 484C is about to aim for in when it was photographed in Nayland in 1980. This Daimler Fleetline/Willowbrook seventy-six-seat bus had been new to another independent operator, Burwell and District, in Cambridgeshire.

Passing William Deaves and Sons, building contractors, in Nayland High Street, *circa* 1978, is Norfolk's SBN 767, heading towards the nearby village of Stoke-by-Nayland. This seventy-seat AEC Regent V with MCW bodywork had been new to Bolton Corporation in 1961 as fleet number 167. The Morris Traveller seen on the left belonged to the late Les Flint, a well-known transport historian.

Norfolk's yard in Nayland always contained something of interest. A visit in mid-1978 revealed 277 AUF, an ex-Southdown Leyland Leopard/Marshall fifty-one-seater, and 69RTO, a former Nottingham City Transport Northern Counties-bodied Daimler Fleetline.

An earlier view at Norfolk's yard, sometime around 1977. Closest to the camera is JUV 537D, a Bedford VAM14 with Duple forty-one-seat coachwork. It had been new to Orange Luxury Coaches of North London. An ex-Aldershot and District Dennis Loline is doing its best to hide from the camera!

Two more Norfolk buses seen at the depot, mid-1989. On the left is NRD 61M, a former Reading Transport 'Jumbo' Bristol VRT/LL6G with Northern Counties H47/29D bodywork, while alongside is ex West Midlands PTE SOE 913H. This Park Royal-bodied Daimler Fleetline/Park Royal had been fleet number 3913 when operating around the Birmingham area.

Seen near its terminus in Stoke-by-Nayland is Norfolk's Coaches' LMA 413T, a Leyland National forty-nine-seater, new to Crosville Motor Services in 1979 when it had been given fleet number SNL413. Richard Huggins photographed it on 4 August 1990; the next year saw Norfolk's being sold to Essex independent Hedingham Omnibuses.

Under the Hedingham ownership, the Norfolk's name was retained for a few years. At the Nayland depot in February 1993 is DWU 294T, given a new-style livery and fleet number L178 in the Hedingham scheme. This Bristol VRT/SL3/6LXB with ECW bodywork, seating seventy-four, had been new as number 1711 in the West Yorkshire Road Car Company.

Although it was an Essex-based company, Hedingham Omnibuses ran a few services into Suffolk. At Bury St Edmunds, laying over in the coach park in spring 1990, is fleet number L126 (BNO 703T). This Bedford YMT with Duple Dominant coach bodywork to grant-aid standards (with folding bus-style doors) had been new to fellow Essex operator Eastern National as number 1217.

Hedingham Omnibuses also served the town of Sudbury, close to the Essex border. On a local route to the housing estates of Great Cornard is L136 (D136 XVW), a Bedford YMQ with Plaxton forty-seven-seat bodywork. It had been bought new in 1987. Hedingham Omnibuses sold out to the Go Ahead Group in 2012 but has, so far, been retained as a separate entity. Sudbury bus station has always had a great variety of operators; vehicles of Beeston's and Felix can be seen.

Another operator to be taken over by Go Ahead (in 2012) was Anglian Buses, a Norfolk-based concern. Services were operated well into Suffolk, as witnessed by KX51 UDJ, a Mercedes 814D with Plaxton bodywork. It was photographed in the Old Cattle Market bus station in Ipswich, in March 2004.

Given fleet number 324, Wright Streetlite WF MX60 BWJ is again seen in Ipswich, outside the railway station on 3 March 2011. This thirty-seven-seater integral bus had been new to Anglian in November of the previous year.

Bures lies on the River Stour to the south of Sudbury. Because the river is the county boundary, the village is divided into two parishes; Bures Hamlet lies to the west, in Essex, while Bures St Mary, in Suffolk, was home to HC Chambers and Son. The company can trace its history back to 1877 though bus services did not start until much later, including the long Colchester–Sudbury–Bury St Edmunds route. On such a duty, in Sudbury *circa* 1973, is XCF 999K, a Willowbrook-bodied Bedford YRQ semi-coach, seating forty-five passengers.

Leaving the depot *circa* 1977, in the centre of the Suffolk portion of Bures, is JRT 710N, a Bedford YRT/Plaxton 'Derwent' fifty-five-seat bus, new to Chambers in 1975.

A two-hour bus journey certainly warrants comfortable seats! The passengers on this Chambers vehicle are well provided for, as it prepares for its departure to Colchester via Sudbury. The service ran hourly, Monday to Saturday, but never on Sundays as the Chambers family were strict Methodists. VRT 840S, a Bedford YMT/Plaxton Supreme Express fifty-three-seat coach, is seen at its northerly terminus, Angel Hill, Bury St Edmunds, *circa* 1978.

Chambers' vehicles seem to have taken over the small bus station in Sudbury on a sunny day in autumn 1983. Closest to the camera is WDX 396X, a Bedford YMT/Duple Dominant B53F, while other Bedford buses seen include bodies built by Willowbrook and Plaxton.

As well as the Colchester to Bury St Edmunds route, Chambers also had some more local services, including one to the Great Cornard Estate near Sudbury. At that town's bus station, in 1994, is E87 KGV. This Leyland Lynx fifty-two-seat saloon certainly made a change from the usual lightweight buses used by Chambers.

Chambers of Bures had operated double-deckers in the 1960s, but by 1972 the fleet was confined to Bedford single-deck vehicles. However, the later years of the twenty-first century saw a return to 'deckers, such as W89 HRT. New in 2000 to Chambers, it is a Scania N113 with rather angular-looking East Lancs eighty-seat bodywork. Operating the Bury St Edmunds to Colchester service, it is seen in historic Lavenham in September 1990.

Chambers also had a few minibuses for local routes. S553 UPV – a Mercedes 814D with Plaxton thirty-one-seat body, new to the company in 1998 – is seen in Sudbury bus station in September 1990.

The later years of Chambers' independent operation saw some second-hand buses enter the fleet. R989 KAR had been new to Dublin Bus, registered 98-D-20395. This Volvo Olympian carries Alexander bodywork, converted from dual-door operation. Behind is another Volvo Olympian, bodied by Northern Counties – P549 WGT, ex-London Central. The photograph was taken in Sudbury bus station on 12 July 2012, just a few months after the takeover by the Go Ahead Group. The Chambers fleet remains in red today, but is managed as part of the Hedingham business.

Carters Coach Services was founded in 1985 at East Bergholt, though the operations were soon moved to Capel St Mary. In the yard at East Bergholt on 18 August 1985 are PWC 344K and SVF 896G. The former is a Bristol RELH6G/Plaxton coach new to Tilling's, an Eastern National subsidiary. The other vehicle came from Eastern Counties in whose fleet it had been number RE896. This Bristol RELH6G with ECW coach bodywork was new in 1969. Photograph by Richard Huggins.

Two more Carters vehicles are seen in the Old Cattle Market bus station in Ipswich on the last day in March 2011. SN51 SXU is a twenty-nine-seat Dennis Dart SLF bodied by Plaxton. It had been new to London United. Alongside is L679 HNV – a Volvo Olympian with Northern Counties bodywork that had been number 679 in the Stagecoach United Counties fleet.

Carters used a modern fleet of buses on their various services in South Suffolk and North Essex. AY07 CUA is an example, seen in Dog's Head Street, Ipswich, on 8 May 2007. This Alexander Dennis Enviro thirty-eight-seater had been received new less than two months before the photograph was taken.

In May 2016, Carters Coach Services was taken over by Ipswich Buses, though retained as a separate entity. On 6 May 2016, only a few days before the takeover, AY60 BVD (given fleet number 280) is seen departing from the Old Cattle Market bus station in Ipswich. New to Carters in 2010, it is a VDL SB180 with MCV Evolution forty-seat bodywork.

Felix Coaches, based at Long Melford, used minibuses on their services in and around Sudbury. Today a low-floor Optare Solo is used to operate these, but on 12 July 2012, a Mercedes Vario 814D registered AY03 BUS is in service. New to Felix Coaches, it carries Plaxton thirty-three-seat coachwork. It is seen in Sudbury bus station, on the town service.

Another operator of minibuses in Sudbury was J. Amos and Son, based at the village of Belchamp St Paul. The company started running buses in 1920 and continued to do so until the last day of 2002. Just over two years prior to this, in September 2000, what was to be the last vehicle in the fleet, D457 YPN, is seen in Sudbury bus station. This Dodge S56/Alexander twenty-three-seater had been new to Brighton Buses.

Goldsmith's of Sicklesmere ran an infrequent stage carriage service into Bury St Edmunds. In April 1990, the regular vehicle, WEX 555S, is awaiting passengers at Angel Hill. The company had bought this Bedford YRQ with Plaxton Supreme Express forty-five-seat bodywork new in 1978. Goldsmith's no longer trade.

Based in the Norfolk town of Thetford, Coach Services Limited operate several services, including three that serve Bury St Edmunds in Suffolk. In that town, on St Andrews Street, Optare Solo thirty-three-seater MW52 PYV is heading for the bus station (despite the destination display) on 26 August 2009.

Far East Travel and its associated company Gemini Travel went into administration in March 2012, with the two services between Ipswich and Framlingham passing to Galloway Travel. On 8 May 2007, GX56 BKY, a Transbus Enviro 200 twenty-seven seater, is seen in Dog's Head Street in Ipswich. The bus had an unusual layout, with doors at the front and rear, as it been a demonstrator for London.

Halesworth Transit traded as Flying Banana, running competitive services in Great Yarmouth. By 28 August 1994, expansion had seen the company running into the small Suffolk town of Beccles, where Richard Huggins photographed H533 KSG. This Carlyle-bodied Iveco 49-10 minibus, seating twenty-five passengers, had been new to a Stirlingshire operator in Scotland. Flying Banana services were sold to First in 1998.

Grey-Green, a very well known London coach operator, ran several express services from the capital to the East Anglian coast. Heading back to London, *circa* 1975, is JHV 494D, a 1966-built Leyland Leopard with fine Harrington 'Cavalier' forty-five-seat coachwork. It is passing along Angel Hill in Bury St Edmunds, probably heading for a comfort break in the nearby coach park.

Petch's Coaches ran a market day service into Bury St Edmunds, terminating at Angel Hill, like many other operators. In the summer of 1980, Bedford VAL14 DUT 456C is ready to depart with a good load of shoppers. This Plaxton-bodied fifty-two-seater had been new to a Leicestershire business, Howlett's of Quorn.

Bickers of Coddenham began running buses in 1927. Expansion came during the Second World War, serving the many RAF stations in Suffolk. By the 1970s, several stage carriage services were operated, mainly based around Ipswich. A fascinating variety of vehicles was on display during a visit in 1976, on an extremely dull day – so apologies are due for the poor quality of this rare photograph. The main subject is a former Guy Special/ECW B26F MXX 356, new to London Transport in 1953, one two in the Bickers fleet. Next to it is former Ipswich Corporation AEC Regal IV BPV 8.

In mid-1978, the large yard at Coddenham behind the Bickers' garage contained 356 EDV. This Bristol SUL4A with ECW thirty-six-seat bodywork had been new to Western National as number 642 in 1951. It was a regular performer on the services into Ipswich.

On the same occasion as the last photograph, ECU 201E was found in the yard of Bickers of Coddenham. New to South Shields Corporation in 1967, this Bristol RESL6L with ECW dual-door forty-five-seat bodywork was purchased by Bickers from Tyne and Wear PTE in 1977.

Another vehicle from the north-east of England in the Bickers fleet, VPT 673L, is seen in the yard in March 1980. It had been new to Gillett Brothers of Quarrington Hill, County Durham, and had passed into the hands of United Automobile Services in 1974. It later went into the ownership of Daisy Bus Services – a Scunthorpe-area operator – before being sold to Bickers in 1979. The bus is an AEC Reliance with Plaxton Derwent fifty-four-seat bodywork.

In 1971, this rare AEC Swift with ECW B45D bodywork was bought new by another Suffolk operator, Lowestoft Corporation, as fleet number 14. GRT 863J is seen in the hands of Bickers of Coddenham at the school in that village, March 1980.

Seen outside a Tolly Cobbold pub, the Blue Coat Boy (since demolished), in Dog's Head Street, Ipswich, in 1980, is Bickers' GGV 47N. This Bristol LH6L, with Plaxton Elite coachwork, seating forty-five passengers, had been new to Bickers in 1974.

A Leyland Leopard in the hands of Bickers of Coddenham, seen at the Old Cattle Market bus station in Ipswich in 1980. 105 CUF, with Marshall bodywork seating fifty-one passengers, had been new to Southdown Motor Services as number 105 in 1963, but was purchased by Bickers from Western National in 1979.

In the latest livery of the time, the spring of 1985, Bickers' RBD 112M is seen in Ipswich's Old Cattle Market bus station. This Bedford YRT/Willowbrook fifty-three-seat bus had been new to United Counties in 1974. Much of the Bickers of Coddenham business was sold to Ipswich Buses in 1988.

Beeston's, a business based in the small Suffolk town of Hadleigh, started out as a haulage contractor in the 1920s. The company started bus operation after the Second World War and has gradually expanded, running several stage carriage services around Suffolk and into Essex. Bought new in 1975 for such duties was LRT 72P, a Bedford YRQ/Duple Dominant with forty-five-seat coachwork fitted with folding doors for bus service operation. It is seen departing from its Crown Street stance in Ipswich, *circa* 1977.

A plastic heron overlooks the parking area at Beeston's garage in Hadleigh during March 1993. Three double-deckers are on display, two being ex-Rhymney Valley District Council Bristol VRT/SL3/6LXB buses bodied by East Lancs, registered GHB 85/6W. Alongside is former London Buses DMS2212 (OJD 212R), an MCW-bodied Leyland Fleetline.

Beeston's of Hadleigh had a considerable coach fleet in the 1980s. In 1983, KBJ 893V was resting in the depot yard. This fifty-three-seat Bedford YMT coach with rare Unicar bodywork was new to the company in early 1980.

An unusual bus in the Beeston's fleet was this Volkswagen LT55 with Optare City Pacer twenty-five-seat bodywork. D369 JUM had been new to London Buses as fleet number OV37. It is seen in the depot yard in February 1993.

Many of Beeston's bus services are centred around Sudbury, where G252 EHD is seen in the small bus station in September 2000. This DAF SB220/Opare Delta forty-nine-seat saloon had been new to a Manchester operator, Wall's of Fallowfield. It is about to depart on a local journey to Great Cornard.

On the same occasion as the above photograph, Beeston's N632 XBU has just arrived from Ipswich on route 91. Again, this bus had been purchased from a Manchester operator, Bullock's of Cheadle, who had obtained this Scania L113CRL/Wright B42F saloon new in 1995.

Another view at Sudbury bus station in the summer of 2000, as Beeston's L518 EHD has just arrived from Great Cornard whilst *en route* to Haverhill. This bus had been new to Quickstep of Leeds in 1994. It is a DAF SB220 with Hungarian-built forty-eight-seat bodywork by Ikarus.

V335 EAK in the fleet of Beeston's of Hadleigh is seen on service in Dog's Head Street in Ipswich in March 2004. This Scania N113DRB with rather angular East Lancs seventy-eight-seat bodywork had been new to a Nottinghamshire operator, Kettlewell's of Retford, in 1999.

Mulleys Motorways was founded in 1938, based at a depot in Ixworth – a pleasant village situated between Bury St Edmunds and Diss. In the mid-1970s, a fascinating fleet was maintained, but the company was best known by enthusiasts for its collection of withdrawn vehicles stored in the yard in various states of repair. Perhaps the best known one was XK 548, an ex-military Locomobile lorry of First World War vintage, converted to an early form of mobile caravan. Alongside is Leyland Tiger PS1/1 CCF 958 new to Mulleys in 1950, with Duple coachwork seating thirty-three. Photograph taken in 1975.

Mulleys had a small fleet of double-deckers intended for school and contract work, though they were occasionally put onto stage carriage duties. Out of use at the depot – *circa* 1978 – is EX 7549, still in its faded Great Yarmouth Corporation livery. As number 49 in that fleet, this all-Leyland Titan PD2/10 had been new in 1953. Two former Hartlepool Corporation AEC Regent V/Roe 'deckers are also seen awaiting their fate.

In contrast to the disused and derelict buses stored in the yard, Mulleys maintained a smart fleet of coaches. In the depot sometime around 1975 are DCF 444L, a Bedford YRT/Plaxton Elite Express fifty-three-seat coach, and XGV 555, a Bedford SB13 with Duple coachwork seating forty-one. Both had been bought new, in 1973 and 1964 respectively.

Given fleet number 77 by Mulleys, RGV111 had been new to the company in 1961. This AEC Reliance has classic Harrington thirty-seven-seat coachwork, photographed in the depot, *circa* 1975.

Mulleys Motorways had two subsidiary fleets, Combs Coaches Ltd and Corona Coaches. In the livery of the latter is OCF 222. This centre-entrance Duple 'Britannia'-bodied AEC Reliance, new in 1960, is seen loading up at Angel Hill, Bury St Edmunds, *circa* 1976.

Illustrating the Combs Coaches operation is STW 666K, a Bedford YRQ/Plaxton Elite Express C45F coach, bought new and seen on service in Sudbury bus station in autumn 1983. Three years earlier, the entire Mulleys business had been taken over, but still retains its operations and separate identity today.

Blue Bus, who also traded as Felixstowe Omnibuses, ran a few services into Ipswich in the mid to late 1980s. Richard Huggins photographed this former Eastern National bus, CVW 858G, at the Old Cattle Market bus station in Ipswich on 10 May 1986. It is a Bristol RELL6G with fifty-three-seat ECW bodywork, which was in the Blue Bus fleet from 1984 to 1989, when it was sold for scrap.

A rare vehicle in the Blue Bus fleet was GSX 112N, a Bedford YRT with Alexander 'Y' type dual-purpose forty-nine-seat coachwork. It had been new to Lothian Regional Transport (Edinburgh Corporation) as fleet number 112 in 1975. It is seen negotiating Turret Lane as it enters the Old Cattle Market bus station in Ipswich in the spring of 1989. The proprietor of Blue Bus gave up Suffolk operations the following year.

Rule's Coaches Ltd went into business around 1920 in the Suffolk village of Boxford, just north from the area known by Dedham Vale, made famous by the painter John Constable. Several stage carriage services were operated, in the Sudbury area. At the company's depot in March 1980 is JKO 671E, an AEC Reliance/Plaxton Panorama forty-one-seat coach, new to Leroy of Tunbridge Wells, Kent. Alongside is a Bedford YRT/Plaxton Elite Express coach, BGV 780L, which had been new to Rule's in 1973.

Also at Rule's Boxford depot in March 1980 is UTL 78. This had been new to another independent, Delaine of Bourne, Lincolnshire, where it had been fleet number 56. This Bedford SB5 had unusual Yeates bodywork to dual-purpose standards, seating forty-four passengers.

Demonstrating the variety in the fleet of Rule's of Boxford, again during a visit in March 1980, is GRT 865J, a rare AEC Swift/ECW combination. It had been new to fellow Suffolk operator Lowestoft Corporation as a forty-five-seater, fleet number 16, in 1971. Rule's Coaches ceased trading around 2000.

Sayer & Son ran a few bus services in and around Ipswich, from a depot on Bramford Road in that town. Operating the 'Urban Circular' service in autumn 1983 is YHA 332J, an ex-Midland Red Ford R192 with forty-five-seat Plaxton bodywork. It is seen passing along Turret Lane through the middle of Ipswich's Old Cattle Market bus station.

The Simonds family started their bus and coach business in 1938. With the closure of most of the railway stations on the Ipswich to Norwich main line in 1966, a replacement bus service was introduced, running from Bury St Edmunds to Norwich and leaving the county of Suffolk just south of Diss. The company's main depot was at Botesdale, to the north-east of Bury St Edmunds, where UKN 203 was photographed in 1978. It is a rare Commer-Harrington forty-two-seat bus that had been new to Maidstone and District as number 8203 in 1955. Simonds had purchased it in 1966, so it certainly had a good, long life!

On the same occasion, at Simonds' Botesdale yard, OUF 521 is sitting in the sun. This Guy Arab IV with Park Royal fifty-seven-seat bodywork, fitted with platform doors, had been new to Southdown as fleet number 521 in 1955.

Simonds certainly liked their Commer vehicles. Sometime around 1978, another one arrives in the depot yard at Botesdale (there was another depot at Diss, in Norfolk). WDL 202, a Commer Avenger IV with Yeates forty-one-seat coachwork, had been new to an Isle of Wight operator, Moss of Sandown, in 1961.

On a sunny day in 1980, Simonds' HBJ 216J is seen resting in the coach park at Bury St Edmunds prior to operating a service to Diss. New to the company in 1971, it is a Ford R192 with Plaxton Derwent bodywork seating forty-eight passengers.

Another Plaxton Derwent body on a lightweight chassis, this time a Bedford YMT, is seen in the Botesdale yard, *circa* 1980. RBJ 46R was bought new by Simonds in 1976.

As dusk falls over Simonds' depot at Botesdale in March 1980, JPV 221N makes ready for an evening journey to Stowmarket. Sixty-six passengers could be seated on this Bedford YRT bus with Duple Dominant bodywork.

Simonds of Botesdale today run into Ipswich, where, at the town's railway station in April 2005, X182 BNH waits for passengers heading towards Diss. This Mercedes 814D, bodied by Plaxton with thirty-one seats, was new to Thames Travel (Wright) of Goring-on-Thames.

The Plaxton Primo integral bus has never proved to be too popular. This one, KX07 KNZ, was originally delivered to Viceroy of Saffron Walden, Essex, in 2007. By 31 March 2011, when photographed in Dog's Head Street, Ipswich, it had passed to Simonds of Botesdale. The twenty-eight-seat vehicle is operating service 113 to Diss, a route that has since passed to Galloway of Mendlesham.

The village of Mendlesham, a few miles north-east of Stowmarket, has been the home of Galloway Coach Travel since 1978, when another independent – Braybrooke's – was purchased. In recent years, several stage carriage service duties have been undertaken, though coaching has been the major *raison d'etre* of the company. Fifty-three-seat DAF coach 2086 PP, built in 1982, is seen in Ipswich, helping out on a bus duty in 1986. The registration of this vehicle was later transferred to a newer Van Hool coach.

For Galloway's bus services, the company purchased N665 JGV new in 1995. This DAF DE02/Ikarus fifty-one-seat saloon is seen in the Old Cattle Market bus station in Ipswich, departing in March 2004.

Galloway Coach Travel really does like the idea of 'cherished registrations', which means a lot of research when writing anything about the history of the company's vehicles. Thankfully it has been possible to ascertain that 1440 PP was originally registered R558 UOT. This Dennis Dart SLF with UVG forty-four-seat bodywork had been new to Marchwood Motorways of Hampshire; it is seen in the layover area of the bus station in Bury St Edmunds on 26 August 2009.

Galloway bought AY09 BYC new in 2009 for use on the company's bus services. The vehicle is a VDL DE02 with forty-five-seat Plaxton Centro bodywork, seen arriving at the Old Cattle Market bus station in Ipswich on 16 April 2009, about a month after delivery.

Galloway's use the railway station front in Stowmarket as the bus terminus in the town. It is here that we see AY55 DGV, with the fine station buildings behind, opened in 1846. The bus is a VDL DE12B with Wright thirty-nine-seat bodywork, photographed on 31 Match 2011.

The registration 2513 PP was originally applied to a double-deck coach owned by County Travel of Leicestershire. However, by the time of this photograph, 19 February 2014, it was firmly attached to this Scania L94UB/Wright saloon in Galloway's fleet. The bus had been new to another East Anglian independent, Anglian Coaches, registered as YR02 ZYL. It is seen in Dog's Head Street, Ipswich.

Squirrells Coaches was founded in the Suffolk village of Hitcham, to the west of Stowmarket, in the mid-1960s. A service was operated into Ipswich, which is where NGV 285M was photographed, at its Crown Street terminus, *circa* 1976. The vehicle is a Bedford YRT/Plaxton Elite Express fifty-three-seat coach, new to the company in 1973, and typical of a rural service vehicle at the time.

At the same location as above, *circa* 1978, is Squirrells' JGV 332N, a Bedford YRT/Plaxton Derwent sixty-four-seat bus, purchased new in 1975.

The date is sometime in March 1980, and a Squirrells of Hitcham-owned bus has reached Crown Street in Ipswich. NBJ 462P is a 1976-built Bedford YRT with sixty-seat Willowbrook body; another bus bought new by Squirrells, in 1976.

Squirrells Coaches are still in business today operating schools, contracts, and private hire, but their stage services passed to Ipswich Buses in January 1989. As part of that transaction, two buses passed to the council-owned operator, one of which is seen here in its new colours, but still with clear evidence of its previous owner. Indeed, JPV 221N is at Squirrells' premises, just prior to the official takeover, on 18 December 1988. The bus, a Bedford YRT/Duple Dominant sixty-six-seater, had been new to another Suffolk operator, Simonds of Botesdale. Thanks to Richard Huggins for this photograph.

Like many Suffolk independents, Theobald's Coaches started running buses in the early 1920s. Based in the small town of Long Melford Theobald's operated in the area around Sudbury, Haverhill and Bury St Edmunds. The company had its main office and garage on the High Street, as seen here *circa* 1977. An ex-Nottingham AEC Renown DAU 364C, one of two in the fleet, is poking its nose out of a cramped yard. Vehicles were often parked in the street or in the former railway station yard.

Another AEC 'decker in the Theobald's fleet, this time a 1960-built Regent V, with MCW bodywork registered LJX 16. It is seen in the depot yard, *circa* 1975. The bus had been new to Halifax Corporation, as fleet number 16.

XGB 779, a 'lowbridge' Leyland Titan PD2/30 bodied by Alexander had been new to a
long-vanished Scottish operator, Smith of Barrhead, in 1959. By around 1975, when this
photograph was taken, it had passed to Theobald's of Long Melford. It is seen passing along
Angel Hill in Bury St Edmunds, on hire to Eastern Counties.

The other former Nottingham AEC Renown, DAU 379C, a Weymann-bodied seventy-seater.
When new it had been number 379 in the East Midlands fleet, which was purchased by
Theobald's in 1976. A year later it is seen in Long Melford High Street, prior to setting out on
a schools run.

Theobald's also sourced some double-deck buses from Maidstone Borough Transport, including JKE 337E, a Leyland Atlantean PDR1/1 with Massey seventy-four-seat bodywork. It is seen in the former railway station yard at Long Melford in autumn 1983.

Sister vehicle to the above, JKE 338E is seen in Constantine Road, Ipswich, on 27 July 1984, operating a special service to and from an event by US evangelist Billy Graham. Thanks to Richard Huggins for this rare photograph.

Theobald's also had some modern vehicles for use on the stage and private hire duties. One of these, LBJ 64P, a Bedford YRT/Plaxton Elite Express fifty-three-seater, new to the company in 1975, is seen outside the depot a couple of years later.

XCF 391K had been delivered to Theobald's in early 1972. This Bedford YRQ with Willowbrook bodywork, capable of cramming in fifty-two seated passengers, is seen in the depot yard in Long Melford, *circa* 1977.

Theobald's of Long Melford purchased LBJ 65P new in 1975 and it became a regular performer on the stage carriage services. It is seen at the depot about to depart on a short run to Sudbury in the autumn of 1983. Fifty-five seats were fitted inside the Duple Dominant bus body, fitted on a Bedford YRT chassis.

On a beautiful sunny day in 1980, Theobald's Bedford YMT/Plaxton Supreme Express fifty-three-seat coach RGV 615R is seen at its Angel Hill terminus in Bury St Edmunds. The company ceased trading before the start of the twenty-first century.

Partridge and Son was the second operator based at the small Suffolk town of Hadleigh. Though some stage carriage work was undertaken, the company's major activity was schools and contract duties. For these, a variety of second-hand vehicles were maintained. Here is a classic example in the fleet, an ex-East Kent AEC Reliance/Park Royal semi-coach, VJG 500, seen in the depot yard in 1978.

Partridge's obviously liked East Kent as a source of second-hand buses. From that company came WFN 830, a 1961-built AEC Regent V with Park Royal seventy-two-seat bodywork, on a piece of hard-standing in front of the depot, 1978.

Many Partridge-owned vehicles were kept in a muddy field behind the main depot. An example, possibly recently withdrawn *circa* 1978, CUW 559C is an AEC Reliance with Harrington Grenadier coachwork, seating forty-one passengers. It had been new to a large London coach operator, Timpson's of Catford.

An unusual coach in the Partridge and Son fleet was NTG 6L, seen parked on the road close to the depot, *circa* 1978. This fifty-seven-seat coach had been new to a South Wales concern, Bebb of Llantwit Fadre. Duple Dominant bodywork is fitted to a Seddon Pennine VI chassis.

As mentioned earlier, Partridge and Son did operate a small amount of stage carriage work and on such duties is MKK 458P, seen in the Old Cattle Market bus station in Ipswich in 1991. New to a Kentish operator, Sonner's of Gillingham, this coach is a Plaxton Supreme-bodied Bedford YRT.

One vehicle that had been new to Partridge and Son was A489 FPV, a Bedford YNT with Duple Laser coachwork. It is seen at the depot in 1983. Partridge and Son sold out to Hedingham and District in 1994 and this coach was last noted with Smiths of Market Harborough around 1995.

Essex operator Regal Busways ventures over the border into Sudbury, where twenty-seven-seat Optare Solo number 205 (YJ58 CDF) is seen on 12 July 2012. Another well-known Essex operator, Stephensons, today runs services in Bury St Edmunds.

Suffolk County Council Education Committee used their minibuses on the occasional normal bus service in Sudbury, such as route number 706. In the year 2000, J81 KBB, a Mercedes 709D minibus, offloads a few passengers – one of whom is clearly of non-school age – in the town's bus station. This vehicle was later sold to Cape Travel of the Penzance area of Cornwall.